The Pray More Challenge

KIMBERLY HARGRAVES

Pray More Challenge by Kimberly Hargraves

Published by Rejoice Essential Publishing
P.O. BOX 75334
Colorado Springs, CO 80970
www.republishing.org

All rights reserved. No part of this book may be used or reproduced by any means, graphic, electronic, or mechanical, including photocopying, recording, taping or by any information storage retrieval system without the written permission of the publisher except in the case of brief quotations embodied in critical articles and reviews.

Unless otherwise indicated, Scripture is taken from the King James Version.

Copyright © 2017 Kimberly Hargraves
All rights reserved

Visit the author's website at
www.kimberlyhargraves.com

ISBN: 1-946756-02-4
ISBN-13: 978-1-946756-02-2

While the author has made every effort to provide accurate internet addresses at the time of publication, neither the publisher nor the author assumes any responsibility for errors or for changes that occur after publication.

DEDICATION

To my Lord and Savior Jesus Christ. First John 4: 19 (KJV) says, " We love him, because he first loved us." John 3:16 (KJV) says, "For God so loved the world that He gave His only begotten Son, that whosoever believeth in Him should not perish, but have everlasting life." First Peter 3:18 (KJV) says, "For Christ also hath once suffered for sins, the just for the unjust, that He might bring us to God, being put to death in the flesh, but quickened by the Spirit."

Contents

Acknowledgments..viii
The Story Behind The Book......................................1
What Is Prayer?..6
Praying Effective Strategies....................................10
What To Do After Prayer..22
Challenge One..27
Challenge Two..30
Challenge Three..33
Challenge Four...35
Challenge Five..38
Challenge Six..40
Challenge Seven...42
Challenge Eight..44
Challenge Nine...46
Challenge Ten...49
Challenge Eleven..51
Challenge Twelve...53
Challenge Thirteen...55
Challenge Fourteen..57
Challenge Fifteen...59

Challenge Sixteen..61

Challenge Seventeen..63

Challenge Eighteen..65

Challenge Nineteen..67

Challenge Twenty...69

Challenge Twenty One..71

Challenge Twenty Two..73

Challenge Twenty Three...75

Challenge Twenty Four...77

Challenge Twenty Five..79

Challenge Twenty Six..81

Challenge Twenty Seven...83

Challenge Twenty Eight..85

Challenge Twenty Nine...87

Challenge Thirty..89

ACKNOWLEDGMENTS

Thank you to everyone who supports this ministry. I am so excited about what God is doing. He has amazing plans for each one of us. I am so glad that you decided to invest in yourself spiritually. Get ready to go higher in God.

ONE
The Story Behind The Book

Welcome to the "Pray More Challenge." You probably got this book for one of the following reasons. You might be struggling in your prayer life and want to improve. You might be super courageous and love challenges. You just want to learn more about prayer and grow in God. Whatever the reason, get ready to be stretched. Be prepared to exercise those spiritual muscles. This book consists of thirty challenges, along with a daily declaration of faith. Before we go into the challenges, we have to cover some basic things to have an effective prayer life and what to do after praying. We want results or answers to our prayers.

So you might be wondering how this book got started. It started back in 2014 when the Lord launched me with an online ministry. I was running away from the call on my life for years. I went to church and sat on the pew for years. I didn't want to serve God or do anything inside of church. I only went to church at that time for my family. I knew God was real, but I did not have a real relationship with him like I do now. Today, the Lord speaks to me every day and I carry His presence. We are very intimate now. This was a long process of many trials and hardships. For years I was confessing Christ with my mouth but He was not in my heart. This is sad but so true because so many other Christians are the same way. They are lukewarm and very carnal. They go to church on Sunday and curse like a sailor and do many other sins Monday through Saturday. I was among the worst sinners.

It wasn't until I got into the wilderness season years ago after losing everything that I finally surrendered. I got on my face and said, "God, I am tired of doing things my way. It is not working anymore no matter how hard I try. I am ready to try things your way now." From that moment, my life began to change. I heard from the Lord more. The Lord began to deliver me from a long battle of anxiety attacks. He began to show me who I was in Him. Then I started to have visitations from the Lord Jesus Christ and other supernatural encounters that are found in the bible. As I submitted to God, He began to give me instructions about the ministry work that I was called to do.

He spoke to me and told me to start a blog. I obeyed, and the blog turned into a book. Now ten books later, we are at the

"Pray More Challenge." When I first begin to write, the Lord was training me how to pray. For years, I was too embarrassed to pray out loud because my prayers were different from everyone else's around me. I didn't like to pray. I remember sweating and shaking every time I had to pray out loud in front of someone. The Lord began to break the fear of praying off me as soon as He launched my online ministry. He gave me an assignment which was to get everyone around me to pray.

I was puzzled and fearful at the same time. I didn't know how I was going to do this assignment. God reassured me and acted as a mother bird pushing her babies out the nest that had to learn how to fly. Then I saw a perfect opportunity to get my social media friends to pray more. There were so many challenges arising on social media at that time. There was the ice bucket challenge where people let someone throw a bucket of ice cold water on them. There was the fire challenge where people let someone put fire on them. The list goes on and on. I noticed that these challenges were demonic and people were getting hurt and even dying behind them. I had enough of crazy challenges around me so in 2014 I launched the "Pray More Challenge."

Here is the original post from the challenge:

"Here's a Challenge that makes sense. This challenge is meant to lead to a life style change. I am tired of seeing dumb challenges. If you don't pray at all, then I challenge you to start praying. If you pray once in a day, then I challenge you to pray twice in a day. If you pray twice a day, then I challenge you to pray three times. If you pray all the time, then I challenge you to pray without ceasing. Let's see and experience a move of God. Who is brave enough to accept this challenge for the next 30 days?"

Many people joined that day. I posted a daily declaration on social media and encouraged my following to pray without ceasing. When I launched my prayer ministry publicly, God showed me that my prayers were powerful and very effective. Many people were blessed from participating in the challenge. Many marriages that were broken were restored. People received salvation. Some people were blessed financially. This lady's grandson who participated in the challenge had his life extended by six months. He was very sick. He was on a mechanical ventilator but our prayers allowed God to get him off the breathing machine for a few months until one day he died in his sleep.

Prayer is so vital because there is a demonic agenda against the church. The enemy has crept in the church and many leaders have compromised and no longer in the will of God. They are in all kinds of sins. God is replacing them with uprising leaders who He can trust to get the job done. There is a demonic attack against our school system. We are seeing increased deaths and bullying among our children. There is a demonic attack against the nation. There is racial tension and sexual orientation confusion. There are increased acts of terrorism that target our food supply all the way to our public transportation. There are so many new emerging diseases that are killing countless people annually.

No matter what the enemy is planning, his plans against God's people will not prosper. God is raising up intercessors and watchmen on the wall to counteract the plans of the enemy. Isaiah 62:6 says, "I have set watchmen upon thy walls, O Jerusalem, which shall never hold their peace day nor night: ye that make mention of the LORD, keep not silence." God needs someone to stand in the gap and pray about everything. Will you be a part of this number that God is calling to pray? So many people are depending on you to pray. One prayer can save a life. I remember years ago, I was suicidal and praying to die. I laid on the couch for three days. I only got up to use the bathroom. I was seeing demonic spirits all around me but I didn't care. I just wanted the pain in life to stop. These spirits were tall and dark and they were hovering over me. A Seer or Prophet who could see in the spirit realm discerned what was going on in my apartment at the time.

She called me and the Lord told me to pick up the phone for her because I wasn't answering any calls. I obeyed the Lord, and she immediately began to pray for me until she seen all those demons leave my apartment. She described them as having red eyes and sharp claws that were trying to claw at me. After she finished praying, I felt so much peace. I thanked her, hung up the phone, got off the couch, and showered. If she didn't pray for me, I probably would be dead. One prayer can stop the attacks of hell. The enemy could plan to kill you one day on your way to work but one simple prayer before you leave the house can sabotage his plans. Do you see why your prayers are needed?

TWO

What Is Prayer?

Prayer is direct communication with God. Sometimes people go to God and just complain about their issues in life. Other people cry out to God for help at the last minute in life when things are falling apart. In this moment, they realize that only God can help. They failed to go to God initially when things were going good. Some people go to God with a long list of things that they want God to do for them. They never ask God, what they can do for Him. Some people go to God in prayer about everything. These people are most likely led by God. Some people just don't pray because they feel like they will bother God and they aren't good enough to pray. We don't get on God's nerves and we don't bother Him. He loves to hear from His children. His Spirit is everywhere.

If someone was in danger, they could call out to God and He would hear them. Psalm 139:7 says, "Whither (Where) shall I go from thy spirit? or whither (where) shall I flee from thy presence?" If someone was sick on their death bed and cried out to God, He would hear them. Years ago when I was in jail, I cried out to God and He heard me. I was suicidal and had no hope to live. Yet in that moment, I felt something I haven't felt in a long time. I felt peace overwhelm me and I gained hope to live life again. Here I was in the darkest time of my life, angry, bitter, and full of hate but God touched me. I was the biggest sinner at that time and God heard my prayer. He began to change my life at that moment.

Prayer should be a two-way conversation between God and us. Most people just do all the talking in prayer and never take the time out to listen. Prayer isn't as complicated as it seems. You can say, "Lord, help me." God will understand. You can fall on your knees and wept uncontrollably and ask God to prove Himself. God will hear you. Some people pray long elaborate prayers. Some people pray simple short prayers. God hears them all. No prayer to God is wasted.

Most people feel like they don't hear from God. If you have the Holy Spirit inside of you, then you can hear from God. God longs to speak to us and He is always speaking. They fail to learn how to still their spirit and focus. They often are distracted in prayer. For instance, their cell phone is going off, and the television is running in the background. If they were to turn off the cell phone and the television and go somewhere quiet, then their chances of hearing God would increase. Taking a notebook and pen to prayer to write down what you hear is taking an act of faith. This is showing God that you expect to hear something from him and He will honor that.

Step number one of taking this challenge is to give your life to Jesus Christ. Years ago, I had a near death experience. I felt like I was about to die. I heard a demonic voice in my head. The devil told me that I was going to die that day. I just shrugged it off and decided to go about my day. It was raining really hard that night years ago. For some reason, I laid the bible on my passenger seat that my sister gave me two weeks prior. After a few minutes of driving, I felt the spirit of death. I knew I was about to die when I got in a bad car accident. Yet, the bible in my car caused heaven to intervene on my behalf.

When all of my CDs and credit cards were scattered across the highway along with broken glass, the bible remained intact. The fire fighter picked up the bible and shook his head in disbelief. He told me, "Here young lady, this saved your life." Then he handed me the bible. I walked away from that car accident without a scratch but one of the people who hit my car wasn't as blessed. He had many injuries. Shortly after that experience, I gave my life to Jesus Christ.

Sinner's Prayer

Lord, I believe that you died on the cross for my sins. Romans 10:9 says, "Because, if you confess with your mouth that Jesus is Lord and believe in your heart that God raised him from the dead, you will be saved. "I make you Lord and Savior of my life. Lord, I desire to have a relationship with you.

Lord, I confess any sins of _____. I repent Lord. Wash me in your blood; in Jesus' name Amen.

Now get connect to a Bible based to church and find someone who can hold you accountable. The angels in heaven are rejoicing now because of your salvation. Luke 15:7 says, "I say unto you, that likewise joy shall be in heaven over one sinner that repenteth, more than over ninety and nine just persons, which need no repentance." Welcome to the body of Christ.If you aren't filled with the Holy Spirit, then pray this prayer. Afterwards, lift up your hands and surrender to God. Then began to praise God by saying Hallelujah over and over again. Just yield and don't think about it. Allow your tongues to change.

Lord, I ask you to fill me with your Holy Spirit. Luke 11:13 says, "If ye then, being evil, know how to give good gifts unto your children: how much more shall your heavenly Father give the Holy Spirit to them that ask him?" Lord, I ask you to honor this word and manifest it now in Jesus name. I will take a step of faith and go praise and worship now. Please let your Spirit overwhelm and saturate me in Jesus name. Amen.

THREE
Praying Effective Strategies

REPENT FIRST BEFORE YOU PRAY

Sin blocks you from receiving answers to your prayers. This is why repentance is so important. Repenting is a behavior change. Often times people confess that they repent but their lifestyle contradicts it. True repentance involves walking away from sinful acts and negative people who will influence you to sin.

2 Chronicles 7:14 says, "If my people, which are called by my name, shall humble themselves, and pray, and seek my face, and turn from their wicked ways; then will I hear from heaven, and will forgive their sin, and will heal their land."

In the following scripture there is a process of getting the answers from God. The end result was healing the land or fixing the situation. Step number one was to humble yourself before God. This involves getting your body in the right posture. Some people lay prostrate on the floor and others pray on bended knees. The next step is to pray as you seek God. Afterwards, repenting is involved or turning from your wicked ways. This means that you can no longer do the sinful things that will be unpleasing to God. When God sees that you have truly repented, He will forgive you and heal your land. This means that He will restore you and perfect whatever concerns you.

PRAY WITH SCRIPTURES

Praying with scriptures is the most effective way to pray. This is praying God's solution to the problem that you are facing. For instance, you may be sick but praying a scripture that says you are healed is praying the solution. You may be poor but the scriptures say you are rich. You may be weary from the storms in life but the word of God says you are victorious. Whatever you are going through, find the scripture that relates to it and meditate on it. It is your responsible to get that scripture inside of you and make it work for you.

Jeremiah 1:12 says, "Then said the LORD unto me, Thou hast well seen: for I will hasten (watching over) my word to perform it." Every time we pray scriptures, God watches over it and will perform it. We have to continue to believe that God is faithful and will deliver on His promises.

Isaiah 55:11 says, "So shall my word be that goeth forth out of my mouth: it shall not return unto me void, but it shall accomplish that which I please, and it shall prosper in the thing whereto I sent it." Your prayers aren't in vain. God will manifest those scriptures in your life as you pray them out.

Psalm 103:20 says, "Bless the LORD, ye his angels, that excel in strength, that do his commandments, hearkening unto the voice of his word." There are angels assigned to you and they do the commands of the Lord. When you pray scriptures, you are praying commands. Put your angels to work. This is why it is so vital not to speak anything negative out of your mouth. Negativity gives the devil power in your life. Proverbs 18:21 says, "Death and life are in the power of the tongue: and they that love it shall eat the fruit thereof." Eat positive fruits or manifested blessings from praying the word of God.

PRAY IN THE PRESENCE OF GOD

Once I did not have any food in my house. I was so desperate for a miracle. I had exhausted all the available resources in my area. The food bank told me they could no longer help me. I was so broken so I fell on my face in prayer. I heard the Lord speak to me. He gave me the instructions to decree the needed scripture in His presence every hour while I was awake. He also gave me instructions to start a homeless ministry. I decreed Philippians 4:19 which says, "But my God shall supply all your need according to his riches in glory by Christ Jesus."

As I worshipped the Lord, His presence was so strong around me and I spoke my decrees faithfully. A few days later, I received a check for $800. I was able to fill up my pantry and refrigerator. I also blessed three families at my local church at the time and feed 100 homeless people. When you speak the word of God in His presence, you are speaking in the anointing. The anointing destroys the yoke of the enemy. This means God's presence destroys the plans of the enemy and brings us liberation. Isaiah 10:27 says, "And it shall come to pass in that day, that his burden shall be taken away from off thy shoulder, and his yoke from off thy neck, and the yoke shall be destroyed because of the anointing."

PRAY IN FAITH

When we pray in faith, it is powerful. There were times in my life when I didn't have anything except for the word of God and my faith. I was hungry and my bank account was in the negative. Yet, I knew deep down inside that my faith in God would not fail. I decided to put God to the test. I prayed, and I knew that something would happen afterwards. God proved me right. God blessed me with an abundance of food and money in my bank account soon afterwards. When I look back on this occurrence, it was supernatural because He blessed me with more money in one day then what I could've made in two weeks working a secular job.

Matthew 21:22 says, "And whatever you ask in prayer, you will receive, if you have faith." Your faith defies all natural laws. You may have received bad news and naturally it may seem nothing will change that. However, if you pray about your situation in faith, God can intervene supernaturally. He can turn your bad news into good news. When you pray about something step out in faith, as if you already have it and praise God in advance.

Hebrews 11:6 says, "But without faith it is impossible to please him: for he that cometh to God must believe that he is, and that he is a rewarder of them that diligently seek him." Your faith is pleasing to God. When you please God, He will favor you and bless you beyond your wildest expectations. When you seek God often and refuse to never give up, great will be your reward.

2 Corinthians 5:7 says, "For we walk by faith, not by sight." We all go through trials in life. We have to trust God over what we see and feel. God is supernatural and His rule reigns over your natural circumstances. Believe God no matter how much it hurts. Your suffering and your faith in God will pay off.

LIVING RIGHTEOUSLY

Psalm 34:17 says, "The righteous cry, and the LORD heareth, and delivereth them out of all their troubles." When you live righteously or uprightly, there is nothing that God will withhold from you. In other words, living a holy lifestyle. Whatever you need, God will provide. If you are in trouble, God will come through. Make a commitment and sacrifice to live right and you will truly be blessed.

BUILDING YOUR RELATIONSHIP WITH GOD

When we focus on God and strive to be more Christ-like God will transform us into the image of His son Jesus. The Holy Spirit will begin to train us and show us how to pray. Years ago, I did not know how to pray. I remember being embarrassed when it was my turn to pray in a small group. Everyone else had scriptures flowing out of their mouths and I didn't know any bible verses to recite. Everyone else prayed with such authority and I prayed with a lack of confidence. After this experience, I made a decision to read and study the bible. I also made a decision to yield fully to the Holy Spirit. It has been a long process of learning how to pray.

God is always showing me new ways to pray as I grow in Him. He constantly reveals new things in His word to me. Years ago, I was in deep worship. My spiritual eyes began to open, and I saw in the realm of the Spirit. I saw a golden bow and arrow laying horizontally shooting arrows. This vision was quite odd because when someone shoots a bow and arrow it's always vertically. I was laying prostrate and pinned to the floor as the Glory of God surrounded me. I heard the audible external voice of God saying, "As long as you remain in the spirit, I will loose my flaming arrows at your enemies."

This vision developed a stronger prayer life in me. The Holy Spirit began to train me how to pray warfare type prayers. He began to show me many weapons in the bible. This led to a television show that the ministry broadcast every Saturday called, "Warfare Strategies". When we build our relationship with God,

He will take us to higher realms and dimensions in the Spirit. Your prayers will become more effective.

REMIND GOD OF HIS PROMISES

If God made you a promise, it may seem like it will never come to pass. This is why reminding God of His promises is so effective. Isaiah 43:26 says, "Put me in remembrance: let us plead together: declare thou, that thou mayest be justified." You can say, "God, you said that I would be blessed with a better job. You sent your prophet or gave a vision about this." If God made you a promise, it will surely come to pass. Continue to remind God of His promises because He is so faithful, and He isn't a liar. Numbers 23:19 says, "God is not a man, that he should lie; neither the son of man, that he should repent: hath he said, and shall he not do it? or hath he spoken, and shall he not make it good?"

BE SPECIFIC

When you pray, don't be afraid to tell God exactly what you want. If you want a new house, don't pray for an apartment. Be specific. If you want to have a girl child, the next time you conceive, then pray about that. When Hannah in the bible prayed to God, she was very specific. She prayed for a male child and that's exactly what God blessed her with (1 Samuel 1).

CONFIDENCE

God wants us to trust him. There were times in my life, my situation was so dark. It seemed like my prayers weren't being answered about some things I needed to happen. But I heard the Holy Spirit telling me to trust him and not to doubt him. Once, my electricity got cut off for one hour. I was blessed that it was only one hour and not cut off for days. During that time, my hours at my secular job in the hospital were cut. I got behind on my utility bill. I had no idea that God was setting me up. I cried and prayed about paying this bill for weeks. God had blessed my friend in New York to have an extra four hundred dollars.

One day she was driving in her city and her car hit a pot hole. This messed up her tire, so she had to go get it fixed. When she went to the car shop to get it fix, they told her that they will fix it for free since it was the city's fault. She had this extra money that she didn't need so she prayed and asked God what to do with the money. God told her to give the money to me. So she text me and asked me what I was doing just as my electricity got cut off. She further inquired and asked if I was okay.

I told her that my electricity got cut off then she took all the information she needed and called the electric company. Within that hour, I praised God with everything within me. When my lights cut back on one hour later, I heard the Holy Spirit tell me not to doubt him. Proverbs 3:26 says, "For the Lord shall be thy confidence, and shall keep thy foot from being (caught) taken." Putting your trust in God will not put you to shame.

1 John 3:20-21 says, "For if our heart condemns us, God is greater than our heart, and knoweth all things. Beloved, if our heart condemns us not, then have we confidence toward God." God wants us to keep our hearts pure. This means to get out

any bitterness or un-forgiveness and other things that would hinder our prayers. Forgive the people who hurt you, bless them and let it go. Once our hearts are pure, we can go to God with confidence in prayer.

HUMILITY

When you humble yourself before God, He will not despise you. You will receive supernatural grace and unmerited favor. Humility is a sign that tells God that you need Him. James 4:6 says, "But he giveth more grace. Wherefore he saith, God resisteth the proud, but giveth grace unto the humble." If you are prideful, then God will oppose you and your prayers will not be answered.

PRAY FOR OTHERS

Whenever you pray to God for someone else's situation while forgetting your own situation, you have passed the selfishness test. We all are going through something in life. We all need God to do something in our lives. If you are seriously in need of a breakthrough, try praying for someone else in need of prayer. During the tough times in life, God will send you someone across your path that is facing the same thing you are facing. Pass the test and pray for them. There is a double portion waiting for you. Job 42:10 says, "And the Lord turned the captivity of Job, when he prayed for his friends: also the Lord gave Job twice as much as he had before." God will get you out of your situation (bondage) just as He did for Job.

FORGIVENESS

One of the biggest prayer blockers is un-forgiveness. We all get hurt and offended by people in life. Our job as children of God is to bless them and pray for them. Matthew 5:44 says, "But I say unto you, Love your enemies, bless them that curse you, do good to them that hate you, and pray for them which despitefully use you, and persecute you." Forgiveness is for you and not the person. The person that hurt you isn't thinking about you and moved on with their life. You are the one that is miserable and losing peace over the situation. This is where the devil comes into your life causing all types of havoc and chaos. Un-forgiveness leads to hate and revenge. Don't take the bait of the enemy and prevent God from answering your prayers. Mark 11:25 says, "And whenever you stand praying, forgive, if you have anything against anyone, so that your Father also who is in heaven may forgive you your trespasses." Un-forgiveness is not pleasing to God.

FASTING

When you pray while fasting, your prayers will be more effective. Fasting is abstaining from all foods. There are different types of fasts such as a complete fast that involves no food; nothing but water. There is a partial fast where you fast for part of the day and not the whole day. There is a Daniel fast where you only eat fruits and vegetables for twenty-one days. There is a dry fast where you eat no food and drink nothing. The list goes on and on. Matthew 6:18 says, "That your fasting may not be seen by others but by your Father who is in secret. And your Father who sees in secret will reward you." Your fasting is not in vain.

We see countless times in the bible when the people had a problem they would fast and pray. God would give them victory. In the book of Ester, Ester did a three day dry fast to get favor with the King when the wicked Haman issued a decree to kill all the Jews. King Jehoshaphat fasted and prayed when three different Kings rose against him. God ambushed his enemies as the dancers who were in front of the army gave him praise (2 Chronicles 20). Fasting with prayer gives the devil two black eyes. Your Spirit man inside you will become stronger as your flesh get weaker during fasting.

TONGUES

When you pray in tongues, you are building up your faith. Jude 20 says, "But ye, beloved, building up yourselves on your most holy faith, praying in the Holy Ghost." There were times when my faith was wavering because of the storm I was enduring. I needed money to pay bills. I needed favor to open up certain doors. It seemed like I needed so much from God. I began to pray in tongues as intensely as I could while pacing the floor and clapping my hands. After I prayed for a while in tongues, I felt stronger in God. I now knew that I was ready to make my decrees. After I made my decrees, I felt like something shifted in the atmosphere. I could feel my situation changing in my favor. A few days later the answers to my prayers manifested.

1 Corinthians 14:2 says, "For he that speaketh in an unknown tongue speaketh not unto men, but unto God: for no man understandeth him; howbeit in the spirit he speaketh mysteries." When we speak in tongues, we are literally prophesying our future. We don't understand what we are praying so we can't mess it up. Praying in tongues is praying in perfect faith because our minds aren't involved. The devil hates when we pray in tongues because he doesn't understand what we are saying. As we allow the Holy Spirit to pray through us, He is praying exactly what we need. Romans 8:26 says, "Likewise the Spirit also helpeth our infirmities: for we know not what we should pray for as we ought: but the Spirit itself maketh intercession for us with groanings which cannot be uttered."

FOUR

What To Do After Prayer

PRAISE

After we prayed about something we should switch over to praise. This is an act of faith. Faith moves the hand of God in our situation. We should praise God in the bad times. Praising God in the bad times is a sacrifice. Your praise is not wasted nor is it in vain. Hebrews 13:15 says, "Through him then let us continually offer up a sacrifice of praise to God, that is, the fruit of lips that acknowledge his name." Our praise unto God is the fruit of our lips. God is pleased with it. Psalm 150:6 says, "Let everything that hath breath praise the LORD. Praise ye the LORD." It is the will of God for us to praise the Lord. It is actually a command. If we don't praise God, then nature will. Luke 19:40

says, "And he answered and said unto them, I tell you that, if these should hold their peace, the stones would immediately cry out." The most powerful thing about praise is that God dwells in it. Psalm 22:3 says, "But thou art holy, O thou that inhabitest the praises of Israel."

BELIEVE

After we prayed, we should expect results. We need to believe that something will happen and things will change in our favor. I remember one time the Lord spoke to me. He said, "Why do you come to me and pray if you will doubt me afterwards." This was my wake up call. God doesn't like it when we doubt. He wants us to know that He is God and He will show Himself strong in our situation. Mark 11:24 says, "Therefore I tell you, whatever you ask in prayer, believe that you have received it, and it will be yours." This is a great promise to stand on when you are believing God for a turnaround. Don't get distracted by what's going on around you. Mediate on the word of God.

Luke 1:45 says, "And blessed is she that believed: for there shall be a performance of those things which were told her from the Lord." The devil's job after we pray is to discourage us and make us doubt God. Don't take the bait. Keep fighting with your faith. You can't afford to be double minded because you will miss out on your blessing. James 1:6-8 says, "But let him ask in faith, nothing wavering. For he that wavereth is like a wave of the sea driven with the wind and tossed. For let not that man think that he shall receive any thing of the Lord. A double minded man is unstable in all his ways."

CLOSE THE DOOR TO SIN

If you compromise your walk with God, then you are forfeiting your blessings and answers to prayers. So many people have received prophetic words about the amazing things God wanted to do in their life but they failed to realize that prophecy is conditional. For instance, God said He would bless them with an amazing opportunity to travel the world. Unfortunately, the recipient fell into sin, fornicated, and died of a terminal disease. Was God a liar? Absolutely not. The word would've manifested if the person would have closed the door to sin by using wisdom and not giving in to temptation. Matthew 26:41 says, "Watch and pray, that ye enter not into temptation: the spirit indeed is willing, but the flesh is weak."

The enemy constantly tempts us with things that are pleasing to our flesh or desires. 1 Peter 5:8 says, "Be sober, be vigilant; because your adversary the devil, as a roaring lion, walketh about, seeking whom he may devour." This why we need to tell negative people goodbye and separate ourselves from bad environments if possible. 1 Corinthians 15:33 says, "Be not deceived: evil communications corrupt good manners." This will cause us to fall away from God if we aren't careful.

COMMAND

Some things we pray about and other things we command to manifest now in Jesus' name. Jesus has given us authority and various commands in the word. Luke 10:19 says, "Behold, I give unto you power to tread on serpents and scorpions, and over all the power of the enemy: and nothing shall by any means hurt you." If the enemy is bothering us, we can command him to leave us alone and get out of our finances, families, businesses, minds, and any other areas in Jesus name. It is up to us to tap into the power of God and walk in the authority Jesus Christ has giving us as His children.

WORSHIP

Worshiping before and after prayer is powerful. Worship draws the manifest presence of God. When we worship something supernatural happens. Our burdens or things we are worried about lift off us in exchange for the peace of God. God begins to heal many inner wounds that we carry as we lift our hands in surrender and worship Him. Right in God's presence is the joy and peace that we desperately need. Psalm 16: 11 says, "Thou wilt shew me the path of life: in thy presence is fullness of joy; at thy right hand there are pleasures for evermore." Once the Lord spoke to me and told me that worship bring in the harvest. That means that you planted seeds of prayers and worship will bring in those answered prayers.

THANKSGIVING

Giving God thanks for something that you haven't even received yet shows you trust Him. You are also activating your faith offering up thanks. It is the will of God to give Him thanks in the good and bad times in life. 1 Thessalonians 5:18 says, "Give thanks in all circumstances; for this is the will of God in Christ

Jesus for you." Thanking God on a daily basis will cause the blessings to flow in your life.

So we covered the basic things. I pray your faith is increased, and you are stirred to receive all God has for you. Let's pray before we begin this challenge as a warmup.

Dear Heavenly Father,

I exalt you. I decree that as I read this book, I will breakthrough in all areas of my life. I decree Micah 2:13 over me that says the breaker is come up before them: they have broken up, and have passed through the gate, and are gone out by it: and their king shall pass before them, and the Lord on the head of them. Lord, manifest this scripture in all areas of my life in Jesus' name. Lord, breakthrough in my finances, relationships, health, and other areas that concern me today. Lord, give me a burden for prayer and allow me to finish this challenge. Thank you, for answering this prayer in Jesus name. Amen.

You can read this book every day as a devotional or straight through. Let the challenge begin.

FIVE

Challenge One

Faith Declaration Of The Day: I will experience a supernatural move of God. I decree and declare that prosperity, increase, promotion, and favor is upon my life in Jesus' name.

Today's Passage: Read 1 Kings 18:41-46

In today's passage we read the story about how the prophet Elijah prayed fervently for it to rain. There was a three-year drought. However, he was a man of faith. He got in a birthing position and prayed. He knew that as he prayed something would happen so he sent his servant to keep checking for rain. This happened seven times and in that moment his servant was able to see a small cloud. Elijah was seeing the rain in the spirit before it manifested in the spirit. He even told the King to go home in faith before it started pouring down raining. Shortly afterwards, the skies darkened and there was a heavy rain fall. God even gave Elijah supernatural power to outrun the chariot of the King.

Maybe you are in a dry season in your life and you need God to send the latter rain. For instance, maybe it seems like you are in time of lack and nothing is working no matter how hard you try. It's time to begin to fervently just like Elijah prayed. The act of Elijah getting into the birthing position is prophetic. He prayed down a miracle and did not stop until it happened. Make a decision to birth out your miracle by intense praying never ceasing until your miracle manifest. Initially, it looked as nothing was happening as he began to pray but he was very persistent. Persistent prayer is vital to your miracle. It took the seventh time for the servant to go near the sea to see a small cloud in the sky.

Do not ever stop praying because there is power in persistent prayer. Elijah believed the command of the Lord when He spoke about the rain. Are you believing the things that God has spoken to you? Are you praying your prophetic words into existence? Elijah took an act of faith by speaking to the King about the rain before there was any proof of it. Are you taking acts of faith towards your miracle? James 2:17 says, "Even so faith, if it hath not works, is dead, being alone." Remember, your faith is pleasing to God so as you step out in faith, God will move on your behalf. Just as God gave Elijah supernatural power to out run the chariot, He will give you supernatural power to pray fervently for your miracle.

Dear Heavenly Father,

I praise your Holy name. I thank you in advance for my miracle. I ask you to increase the spirit of prayer in my life so I can pray fervently and effectively. Lord, send the latter rain on my situation in Jesus name. I decree and declare that my prayers are powerful and great things are happening even now as I pray. I proclaim that I will not stop praying until something happens in Jesus name. I take an act of faith today and I will speak my miracle into existence in Jesus name. Thank you, for answering this prayer in Jesus name. Amen.

SIX

Challenge Two

Faith Declaration Of The Day: I decree my prayers are changing things around me. I declare Psalm 20:4 today that the Lord is giving me the desire of my heart and making all my plans succeed in Jesus' name.

Today's Passage: Read 1 Kings 18:20-40

In today's passage we read the story about how the prophet Elijah challenged the false prophets. He wanted them to prove that their god Baal was real and he would prove that His God was the true God. He was very bold, and he challenged all 450 prophets of Baal. The test to prove which God was real was to get the true God to send fire out the sky and burn up their offering. The prophets of Baal cut up a bull and placed it on an altar and called to their god but there was no answer. They even danced and worship all day but still no answer. Elijah mocked them. Now it was Elijah's turn to make an altar unto His God. So he even went so far to drench his meat offering and the altar with water three times.

He even filled the surround ditch with water. He wanted to prove that God could set fire to this offering no matter how wet it was. He prayed that God would show that He was the true God and immediately fire came from heaven and burned the sacrifice, the stones, and the ground around the altar. The water in the surrounding ditch dried up as well. When the people saw what happened they fell to the ground confessing that Elijah's God was the true God. Afterwards, Elijah killed all the prophets of Baal.

Your faith may be tested right now? You may be in a challenging position and you need God to prove Himself to you. God is so faithful and He will fulfill every promise that He made to you. Just as Elijah set up an impossible situation by saturating the offering with water so it would not be easily lit with flame, God can touch your impossible situation. God is bigger than your life's problems. Nothing is too hard for him. If God made a promise to you, then He is obligated to bring it to pass as long as you follow His commands. God specializes in miracles and He will get the Glory out of all impossibilities. Elijah prayed that God would show that He was real. God honor his prayer and answered by fire.

You can also have the God who answers by fire move in your life and situation. Just as the people fell down to the ground after witnessing this great miracle, so will you when God blesses you.

You will praise God as never before when He does a miraculous work on your behalf. Elijah killed and got rid of the problems, deceptions, falseness, or the prophet of Baal. God will kill, eliminate, and destroy all the problems, deceptions, falseness in your life as you trust Him. Don't stop praying because the God who answers by fire is listening.

Dear Heavenly Father,

You are worthy. I repent of my sins and I humble myself before you. I ask you to prove your power in my life. I ask you to honor your word and manifest it in Jesus name. I decree and declare that I will not give up seeking you until I receive my answer. I decree that my prayers are availing much. I decree that you will answer the simplest prayers just as you did for Elijah. God, I thank you in advance for giving me the victory in Jesus name. Amen.

SEVEN

Challenge Three

Faith Declaration Of The Day: Since I am the righteousness of God, I decree that my prayers are availing much (James 5:16). I decree and declare Proverbs 16:3 that as I commit my works to the Lord, my plans will be established in Jesus' name.

Today's Passage: Read Exodus 32:7-14

In today's passage we read the story about how the prophet Moses was able to intercede on the people's behalf. These people were rebellious. Moses went up to the Mountain for a while to seek God but the people became impatient and didn't know where he went. They talked Aaron who was Moses' prophet into making them a golden calf or idol. They began to worship the idol, drink alcohol, and commit sexual sins. God hates idols. He commanded the people to only serve Him. They turned their back on God and forsook His laws. God was so angry that He was ready to destroy these people for their stubborn and rebellion. However, Moses prayed and reminded God of the covenant promises He made. In that moment, God changed His mind.

Maybe you are in a difficult situation. Just as Moses prayed and reminded God of His promises so can you. God is so merciful, and He loves us with an everlasting love. He is also the God of multiple chances. As you pray God's word back unto Him he will remember His covenant and come through for you. God can change His mind about your situation. He can decide that today is the day for Him to act on your behalf because you have placed your full trust in Him. You can also intercede for your loved ones and just as God changed His mind with the Israelites He can do it for your family. Remember, the word of God is powerful, and it is truly alive. Don't ever stop interceding for others because someone's life is depending on it. The power of intercession is life changing.

Dear Heavenly Father,

I will praise you. I repent of my sins. I humble myself in your presence. I ask you to move mightily in my life and those who are also connected to me. Lord, I ask you to honor your covenant of peace, prosperity, and fellowship with me. I will continue to remind you of your promises because I know your word will not disappoint me. I thank you for your mercy and grace. Lord, bless me and my loved ones to stay in your will. In Jesus name Amen.

EIGHT

Challenge Four

Faith Declaration Of The Day: I declare Philippians 4:19 over my life that God is supplying all my needs according to his riches in glory by Christ Jesus. God is my refuge and strength, a very present help in trouble (Psalm 46:1).

Today's Passage: Read 2 Kings 20:1-11

In today's passage we read the story about how the prophet Isaiah was sent to King Hezekiah. God told him to tell Hezekiah to get his house in order because he was going to die. Hezekiah had been very sick but after he received the word from the prophet, he turned his face to the wall and begin to pray. He asked God to remember him because he had always obeyed him and giving God his whole heart. Then he wept bitterly or cried loudly.

Isaiah was on his way out in the courtyard, but God spoke to him. He was commanded to go back to Hezekiah to deliver a new word. God spoke through Isaiah and said He had heard his prayer and seen his tears, fifteen years will be added unto his life, and he would save the city from the hand of the enemy or the Assyrian King. Hezekiah followed the instructions of the prophet but he needed a sign from the Lord that He would be made well. Isaiah prayed, and the Lord brought the shadow ten degrees backwards.

Have you recently received bad news? Maybe you have been oppressed for a long time. Perhaps you are seeking God for a sign for your life. God will always confirm His word with multiple witnesses. Just as God changed his mind about Hezekiah and extended his life, he can change his mind about you. You may be terminal but God is more powerful than sickness or death. If God gave Hezekiah more time why can't he do it for you? It starts with obedience to God's word and loving him with your whole heart. Hezekiah was devoted and faithful to God. As you obey God, love him, and remain faithful to him, He will move mightily on your behalf. Hezekiah cried and prayed with all of his heart reminding God of his faithfulness and immediately God moved. Your tears are prayers too. Sometimes, the pain is too intense to pray with words. God understands, and He is watching and listening. Nothing is too hard for God.

Dear Heavenly Father,

I reverence you. I come before you and give you all of me. I repent of my sins today. I give you my pain and brokenness. Sometimes,

I cry because of the trials but I know that you understand my prayers. Lord, I am so thankful that you have kept a list of my tears and put them in your bottle. I ask that you remember me and move mightily in my life just as your moved for King Hezekiah. I vow to you this day to remain faithful and to follow your every command. Thank you, for answering this prayer. In Jesus name. Amen.

NINE

Challenge Five

Faith Declaration Of The Day: Today I declare God's explosive blessings over my life. I will cast my cares on The Lord and he will sustain me; He will never let the righteous be shaken (Psalm 55:22).

Today's Passage: Read Exodus 32:30-34

In today's passage we read the story about how the prophet Moses went to God to get the people's sins atoned. They had just committed a terrible sin by worshipping the golden calf. Moses was so mad that he threw the two tablets or stones that the ten commandments were written on breaking it. He interceded for the people because He knew that God was ready to judge the people. Moses asked God to forgive them. He prayed boldly to God saying, "Lord, if you don't forgive them then blot my name out of your book." But God responded saying, "He would only blot the names that have sinned against him and he would punish the people in His timing."

We need to stand in the gap for others especially the nation's sin. We can boldly ask God to forgive us all. God is ready to judge the wicked every day. However, our intercession for their salvation and deliverance can make all the difference. Moses stood in the gap and intercede for the people when they sinned. God doesn't want anyone to perish. Yet he will judge the people for their disobedience and sins. Someone prayed for you while you were in the world. Return the favor and pray for the lost souls. Decreeing salvation over the lost is powerful because it will be established in the heavens. No matter how bad things seem around you, do not stop praying. God is so faithful, and He delights in the prayers of the righteous.

Dear Heavenly Father,

I thank you for your grace and mercy. I repent of my sins and the sins of the people in this nation. I am asking you for forgiveness this day. Save the lost. I pray that you would send conviction on the wicked and they would truly repent. Lord, draw them near to you and soften their hearts towards the gospel of Jesus Christ. I decree that my household would be saved as well. Thank you, for answering this prayer in Jesus name. Amen.

TEN

Challenge Six

Faith Declaration Of The Day: I decree that when I pray, I am in direct communication with God. Today I declare Proverbs 8:35 over me that I shall obtain the favor of the Lord. No good thing does he withhold from those who walk uprightly (Psalm 84:11).

Today's Passage: Read Acts 12:1-16

In today's passage we read the story about how King Herod arrested Peter and put him in jail. Herod planned to bring Peter to trial after the Passover feast. As he was in jail, the church prayed earnestly for him. The night before the trial, an angel appeared in his cell and his chains fell off. He got dressed. Amazingly, he was able to sneak pass the soldiers who were guarding the jail cell. He was able to get pass the gates. God sent His angel to rescue him because of the prayers of the saints. Peter went to the exact house where the people were praying for him at that exact moment. They were amazed.

Do you need a miracle? Just as God showed up for Peter supernaturally and did the impossible, so will He do it for you as you continue to pray earnestly. When God is in the midst of your circumstances, things will not always make sense. Peter couldn't perceive whether the angel was real or in a vision initially. However, he soon realized that God had sent an angel of deliverance. God rescued him suddenly right before his trail. God will rescue you suddenly too right before your deadline. Remember the natural mind can't comprehend the things of the spirit. Turn your mind off and believe God. Don't try to figure how things will come together. As you pray in faith, God will come through for you supernaturally.

Dear Heavenly Father,

I praise you. I repent of my sins. I am so encouraged when I read about how you freed Peter from prison. I ask that you free me from every demonic oppression and stronghold in Jesus name. I know that there is liberation in your presence so that's where I will dwell. I decree that I will press into worship and praise and surrender my doubts and worries. I thank you in advance for you answering my prayers. I know you are moving on my behalf as I pray earnestly in Jesus name. Amen.

ELEVEN

Challenge Seven

Faith Declaration Of The Day: I decree that as I go through trials in life and face difficulties, I will keep my mind stayed on Jesus and he will keep me in perfect peace (Isaiah 26:3). Today I declare that I will experience God's faithfulness so I do not have to worry or doubt. I will trust God because His word will not disappoint.

Today's Passage: Read Genesis 18:22-33

In today's passage we read the story about how prophet Abraham was about to intercede for the city of Sodom. Abraham was God's friend. God didn't want to destroy Sodom until He told Abraham His plans. The city of Sodom was overall very wicked. Yet, Abraham asked God several questions. He knew that God was merciful and just, so he asked if God would destroy the few righteous in that city along with the wicked. Abraham started off asking God if there were fifty righteous all the way to ten righteous people in the city, would God destroy it? God had compassion and agree if there were ten righteous people found, then He would not destroy the city.

The closer we are to God the more insight we will have when it comes to intercession. In the realm of intercession is where we can feel the burden of the Lord and burdens of others. God wants to trust you with revelation and various secrets. Just as Abraham was able to stand before the Lord and plead for the people who live there, you can stand before the Lord and intercede for others as well. God is love and His mercy is great. Your prayers can prevent someone from dying. Remember someone prayed for you when you were sinning in the world. One prayer can cause heaven to intervene in someone's life. Continue to pray for the lost souls to be drawn near to God and that they will confess Jesus Christ as Lord.

Dear Heavenly Father,

I exalt you. I am so thankful that you never gave up on me. I decree and declare that I will posture myself in deep intercession. Lord, reveal to me what I need to pray for or who I need to pray for. I totally submit to you. I am willing to allow you to use me to be a watchman on the wall. I will sacrifice and invest time in prayer because I know it's not in vain. Lord, I know someone out there is depending on my prayers to receive salvation, healing, or deliverance. Thank you, for answering this prayer in Jesus name. Amen.

TWELVE

Challenge Eight

Faith Declaration Of The Day: I decree that I will keep on pressing on as I pray. In my distress I cried unto the Lord, and He heard me (Psalm 120:1). If I ask anything according to His will, He hears me (1 John 5:14). I declare that God will open new doors of opportunities and set His favor upon me in Jesus' name.

Today's Passage: Read 1 Kings 3:5-14

In today's passage we read the story about how King Solomon went to a place of worship and offered a 1,000 burnt offerings. While he was there, the Lord appeared to him in a dream asking whatever he wanted He would give to him. Solomon asked for wisdom to be King, to lead the people effectively, and to discern between evil and good. God was pleased with his answer and gave him things he didn't ask for such as honor, riches, and a long life. Prayer is a conversation with God and God can speak to you in dreams. Your sacrifice will get God's full attention.

If you are about God's business, then he will be about your business. In other words, if you make God your first priority, then he will bless you with things that are important to you without you even asking for it. So many times in life we place temporal things or material things before spiritual things. However, if we seek the things of God, He will always provide us with material blessings. Praying for wisdom and spiritual things are pleasing to God. God will not reproach you and He will give you a generous supply.

Dear Heavenly Father,

I will praise you. I repent of being selfish and placing my agenda before yours. I ask you to forgive me. I pray that I will decrease and you will increase in my life. I decree and declare that I will die to self and take up my cross daily. Lord, lead me and guide me. I will follow after you. I will submit to your plans for my life. I desire wisdom and spiritual gifts. I decree that I will sacrifice my time, offerings, fasting, worship, and praise. Lord, have your way in my life in Jesus name. Amen.

THIRTEEN

Challenge Nine

Faith Declaration Of The Day: I will enter into his gates with thanksgiving, and into his courts with praise: I will be thankful unto him, and bless his name (Psalm 100:4). I declare Psalm 37:4 that I would delight myself in the Lord, and he will give me the desires of my heart.

Today's Passage: Read Psalm 22

In today's passage we read the prayer by King David when he was suffering. He felt like God had forsaken him because God felt so far away. He was discouraged because it seemed like nothing was happening when he prayed and that God wasn't hearing his prayers. He began to praise God and remembered how God came through for his ancestors. David was being mocked. He was hated by his enemies. They even ridiculed him about him serving God. He reminded God that He has been with him since he was born. He felt weak, and he had lost so much weight that his bones were showing through his skin. He vowed to God that if He would save him, then he would give Him praise and tell others about Him. David had to encourage himself when he was suffering.

There are many times in life where we feel lonely and forsaken. However, that is not true. God is always there even when we cannot perceive him. His spirit is omnipresent. Sometimes at the darkest moments, it seems as the suffering is unbearable. It is in this moment where we have to reflect on God's goodness and encourage ourselves. When we remind ourselves of God's promises and read various testimonies, our faith in God is strengthened. We all have to suffer in different seasons of our lives but God will get the Glory out of it. Jesus Christ had to suffer on the cross for our sins. He even felt like God had forsaken him. You may seem like life is hopeless but God will turn it around as you cry out to him. Never feel ashamed to come to God broken. He will not despise you in your suffering. As you cry out to God, you will begin to experience His presence and peace.

Dear Heavenly Father,

I lift up your name. I humble myself. I repent of all my sins. I ask for forgiveness. Lord, have mercy on me. I come to you broken, pouring out my heart. The suffering I am enduring is great and I need a release. I release these burdens unto you. I know you are faithful. I know you will get the Glory out of my pain. I know that you will bless me. I know that I will have a testimony. Give me peace, joy, and strength. I thank you in advantage for moving mightily in my circumstances in Jesus name. Amen.

FOURTEEN

Challenge Ten

Faith Declaration Of The Day: I will be encouraged today. I will cast my cares upon God because He cares for me (1 Peter 5:7). I declare Ephesians 2:7 that God might show the exceeding riches of His grace in His kindness toward me through Christ Jesus.

Today's Passage: Read Psalm 57

In today's passage we read the prayer by King David when he was troubled. Perhaps he was being pursued by Saul and running for his life. He calls out to God for mercy and asks for protection. He recognizes God's supremacy, and that He was the source for everything. He prays to God about his enemies but chooses to praise Him. He didn't focus on his troubles but he chose to focus on God. He knew that God would get the Glory out of his troubles.

Whenever we get in trouble in life, we need to focus on God and not our problems. Whenever we focus on our problems, we become worried and rarely nothing changes. Yet when we focus on Jesus, we have peace and things supernaturally changes. Sometimes, things in life are out of our control. No amount of worrying or taking matters into our own hands are able to solve the problem. God is so faithful and will provide you protection as you cry out to Him. He is your refuge in the troubled times. Make a decision to fully trust God and watch Him bring you to a place of deliverance.

Dear Heavenly Father,

I glorify your name. I repent and I cry out for mercy. You see what I am going through and I need your help. I pray a hedge of protection around me in Jesus name. Lord, give your angels charge over me in Jesus name. Lord, I realize that you are my source for everything in life. I ask that you give me strength to endure the storm in Jesus name. I decree and declare that I will not give up. I proclaim that I am victorious. I thank you Lord for fighting all my battles in Jesus name. Amen.

FIFTEEN
Challenge Eleven

Faith Declaration Of The Day: I will press through and continue to pray no matter what opposition comes my way. I will be encouraged. I decree Psalm 139:14 that I will praise God because I am fearfully and wonderfully made. I pray that my soul blesses God and I do not forget all His benefits.

Today's Passage: Read Luke 18:9-14

In today's passage we read a parable told by Jesus Christ. There were two men in this story. One person who was a Pharisee or a religious leader and the other man, a tax collector. The Pharisee was self-righteous and looked down on others. He prayed a very self-centered prayer, exalting himself. He was a very prideful man. The tax collector, humbled himself and prayed a prayer of repentance. God accepted the tax collector's prayer over the

Pharisee's prayer. God will never despise your prayer if you come to him in humility.

The tax collector knew he needed God. He confessed his faults before the Lord, crying out for mercy. It is good to come clean before the Lord and just be honest. We aren't supposed to think of ourselves more highly than we ought to because we all have flaws. God is not impressed by religious acts when your heart is not pure before him. If you humble yourself God will exalt you. Contrarily, if you exalt yourself, you will be humbled. Once, you humble yourself in prayer and truly repent of your sins, you will begin to see God answer your prayers as never before.

Dear Heavenly Father,

I humble myself before you. I am tired of being outside of your will. I am ready to try things your way. My way is not working out. Have mercy on a sinner like me. I confess all of my sins and I truly repent. I ask you for forgiveness. Lord, create in me a pure heart. I decree and declare that I will walk uprightly before you. I confess that Jesus Christ is Lord and Savior. I ask Jesus to rule in my heart today. Thank you for answering this prayer in Jesus name. Amen.

SIXTEEN

Challenge Twelve

Faith Declaration Of The Day: I decree and declare that I will not become weary in well doing because at the proper time I will reap a harvest if I do not give up (Galatians 6:9). Today I declare Deuteronomy 28:1-2 that I may obey God's commandments and all His blessings shall come upon me.

Today's Passage: Read Acts 22:4-16

In today's passage we read the story about Paul. He taught he was in the will of God by persecuting the followers of Jesus Christ. He was very zealous to the point where he killed Christians and put some of them in jail. So one day he was near Damascus and a bright light blinded him. Immediately, he fell to the ground as he heard a voice asking why are your persecuting me? Paul asked who the voice was. The voice identified himself as Jesus

Christ of Nazareth. Paul asked another question, what shall I do, Lord? Then Paul received his instructions to the right pathway.

Paul obeyed and met a prophet named Ananias who prayed for his sight to return. When you are in prayer, it is okay to ask God questions. It is better to seek God and receive answers for your concerns then to get out of His will for your life. Every day, we should ask the Lord to guide us. Oftentimes, we come to God with our concerns and never take the time to listen. Prayer is two-way communication. Take time today and ask God What He wants for you and what instructions he needs you to follow.

Dear Heavenly Father,

I exalt you. You are so great. I humble myself and repent of my sins. I ask you for forgiveness. I also forgive and bless anyone who has hurt me. I bring my concerns to you and lay them on the altar. I trust that you will work my problems out. I thank you in advance for the manifestations of my prayers. Lord, what is your will for my life? What do you want me to do today? I am laying before you and will take the time to listen now. In Jesus name. Amen.

SEVENTEEN

Challenge Thirteen

Faith Declaration Of The Day: I decree that I will keep pressing forward as I pray. My prayers are not in vain. God will grant me the desires of my heart for my extra effort. Today I declare 3 John 1:2 that all may go well with me and that I may be in good health, as it goes well with my soul.

Today's Passage: Read Acts 4:23-31

In today's passage we read the story about Peter, John, and the believers. Peter and John were persecuted for preaching the gospel of Jesus Christ. There was a man that got healed before the religious leaders' very eyes. They could not deny the miracle that they witnessed. They threw Peter and John in jail but had to release them. They wanted to punish them severely, but the people were glorifying God because of the miracle of healing that took place. The religious leaders asked Peter and John to not preach in the name of Jesus but they refuted.

Eventually, they meet with the believers and told them what had just occurred. The believers started exalting God in prayer reminding Him about all the persecution and plans of the enemy to stop the gospel. Then they asked God to make them bold and to release signs and wonders. After they prayed that prayer God moved in a mighty way and filled everyone with the Holy Spirit. Just as the believer's prayers shook up the atmosphere so can your prayers as well. As you pray for boldness and miracles to be released, God will extend His hand in your situation.

Dear Heavenly Father,

I exalt you. You made heaven and earth. Your works are perfect. I am in awe of your righteous acts. No matter how the enemy tries to attack me, it will never work. No matter how the enemy tries to stop your plans, it will never work. No weapon formed against me will prosper. You are sovereign and you reign supreme. You are more powerful than the enemy in Jesus name. I plead the blood of Jesus upon me and everything that concerns me. Lord, make me bold so I can preach the gospel with authority. Lord, release many signs, wonders, and miracles in my atmosphere. Thank you for answering this prayer in Jesus name. Amen.

EIGHTEEN

Challenge Fourteen

Faith Declaration Of The Day: My prayer is communication with God. God is my refuge and strength, a very present help in trouble (Psalm 46:1). Today I declare Mark 11:24 that whatever I ask in prayer, I believe that I have received it, and it will be mine.

Today's Passage: Read Daniel 9:1-19

In today's passage we read the story about the Prophet Daniel. He was a great man of prayer. He was read the prophecies from prophet Jeremiah. Daniel prayed a prayer of intercession for his nation. He was standing in the gap. Israel was in captivity by the Babylonians because of their disobedience. He came to God repenting for the sins of the nation. He asked God to forgive them for their wicked ways and to turn His anger from them.

He cried out for mercy and reminded God that Israel was His chosen people.

In today's society, it seems as the hand of the Lord is against certain nations. They have sinned against Him and forsaken His commandments. Just as Daniel interceded for his nation, so can you. You can go boldly to God and remind him of all his promises. You can also cry out for mercy and forgiveness for your city and nation. Your region is depending on your prayers to bring the desired changes you want to see. Make a decision to stand in the gap because every prayer counts.

Dear Heavenly Father,

Oh, great is your mercy. You are so just. I humble myself today. Lord, we have transgressed against you and forsaken your ways. Often times, we have rebelled against you. You are so Holy. I ask you to have mercy upon this nation and forgive us for our wicked ways. Lord, turn your anger away from this nation. Lord, purge us and sanctify us with the blood of Jesus Christ. Lord, bless this nation to obey your commandments. I decree the people's hearts will be receptive to the gospel of Jesus Christ. Thank you for answering this prayer in Jesus name. Amen.

NINETEEN

Challenge Fifteen

Faith Declaration Of The Day: Praise the Lord! I am halfway through this challenge. My prayers are powerful but more effective when I pray using scriptures. I pray that God will give me leaps and bounds in all areas of my life. Today I declare Isaiah 61:3 that God will give me beauty for ashes, the oil of joy for mourning, and the garment of praise for the spirit of heaviness.

Today's Passage: Read Luke 1:46-56

In today's passage we read the story about when Mary went to go see her cousin Elizabeth. Elizabeth began praising God when her unborn child jumped for joy inside her when Mary came to visit. Elizabeth reminded Mary that she was surely blessed. Mary replied with a prayer of humility and thankfulness. She knew that everything good pertaining to her was because of God. She began to exalt God.

A simple of prayer of thankfulness is very powerful. It shows God that you appreciate Him. It is also an act of faith to thank God for the things to come. Your situation may be dark right now but as you began to humble yourself and thank God, you will experience a turnaround. Just as Mary and Elizabeth were filled with the joy of the Lord, so will you. Begin to exalt God and thank him for all the promises he has made to you.

Dear Heavenly Father,

You are awesome. You have done so many wondrous acts all throughout the earth. I know that you are faithful even when I am not. I humble myself and repent of my sins. I exalt you. I am so thankful. I refuse to focus on the negative things but instead, I will look to you. Your promises constantly give me hope. Lord, fill me with joy, peace, and hope today. I thank you in advance for my breakthrough in Jesus name. Amen.

TWENTY

Challenge Sixteen

Faith Declaration Of The Day: I will not underestimate the power of prayer. I am a living witness of the power of prayer. Today I declare that I am anointed and a powerful person of God. I declare that I am a doer of the Word of God and a channel for his blessings.

Today's Passage: Read Luke 22:40-46

In today's passage we read the story about how Jesus prayed in the Garden of Gethsemane on the night before He was crucified. He was praying for strength against temptation. He knew what his purpose was, but he yielded himself to God's will. Angels had to come to strengthen him so he could fulfil his assignment. Jesus was in agony but he continued to pray even harder. He was sweating to the point where his sweat is compared to drops of blood. He knew the importance of his mission and he refused to give up.

You may be in anguish and don't understand the suffering you may be enduring. As you press forward in prayer, God will send angels to come strengthen you. You may not see them or be aware of them but they do the Lord's bidding. The easiest way to get through the trials in your life is to totally surrender your will and yield to God's will for your life. Your situation may seem impossible but God will work it out for you. Don't give up. Remember to always pray so you will not fall into temptation.

Dear Heavenly Father,

You are so worthy. I come before you and I give you me. Take the pain and brokenness. Not my will Lord, but your will. I don't understand why I have to suffer sometimes but I choose to believe that you are working things out. Lord, strengthen me so I can fulfil my assignment. Lord, I decree that I will die to myself daily and put on Jesus Christ. I just want to please you and stay in your will. Bless me God and remember me. Thank you for answering this prayer in Jesus name. Amen.

TWENTY ONE

Challenge Seventeen

Faith Declaration Of The Day: As I pray, I am a building a strong altar. The more I pray the stronger my altar. I will be like the house built on a rock in the parable in Matthew 7. My house will be strong enough to keep standing regardless of what storm comes my way. Today I declare that God's favor surrounds me like a shield.

Today's Passage: Read Matthew 6:9-13

In today's passage we read the Lord's prayer. We see an example on how the Lord told us how to pray. The religious leaders were very hypocritical with their prayers. They did not pray in secret to God but they prayed in public to be seen by men. When they did pray, the used vain repetitions and big words trying to make their prayers sound more elaborate. Jesus prayed that God's will be done on earth as it is in heaven. He also prayed that we forgive one another just as God has forgiven us. The Lord's prayer is the ultimate example of a selfless prayer.

Just as the disciples wanted Jesus to teach them how to pray, the Holy Spirit can teach you as well. The Holy Spirit will lead you and guide you into all truth. If you totally surrender to Him and submit to His plans, you will be transformed and inspired. Overtime you will notice how your prayers went from being self-centered to Christ-centered. Your attitude will change from being ungrateful to being grateful as you grow spiritually. You will no longer fret about the small things in life.

Dear Heavenly Father,

I exalt you. I repent of my sins. I ask you to help me on this journey. I don't want to be selfish or self-centered in my prayers. Show me the best way to pray. Strengthen my prayer life. Lord, you are compassionate and full of love. You have grace on the humble. You bless those who have compassion on the poor and count others more significant than themselves. I decree that as I pray and bless others, you will bless me. Thank you for answering this prayer in Jesus name. Amen.

TWNETY TWO

Challenge Eighteen

Faith Declaration Of The Day: I will press on as I pray. I will take some time to listen to the voice of Almighty God by being still in his presence. Prayer is a two-way communication. Today I declare Numbers 6:24-26 that the Lord will bless me and keep me; the Lord will make His face to shine upon me and be gracious to me; the Lord will lift up His countenance upon me and give me peace.

Today's Scripture: Read Luke 23:34

In today's scripture we read the about Jesus was on the cross being crucified. The soldiers and the people mocked him. They said that "He can save others but He can't saved himself." They even threw dice or cast lots deciding who would take his clothes. They made fun of him being the Messiah. Jesus prayed for them asking God to forgive them. This one of the simplest prayers to pray for someone who is persecuting you. The person will need God's mercy one day for reaping what they have sown.

Praying forgiveness for people who hurt you is a very hard thing to do for some people. Most people want the person who hurt them to suffer and pray the price. However, Jesus gave us a good example of God's love. He had God's love flowing through his veins that he didn't take it personally that they persecuted him. He made a choice to forgive and let it go. He looked at the ultimate plan which was redemption of mankind. Remember, forgiveness is for you and not the person who hurt you. You don't want anything to block your blessings. Make a choice to let it go today!

Dear Heavenly Father,

I reverence you. I come before you as humble as I know how. I confess that many people have hurt me. I realize that forgiveness is a choice. If Jesus could forgive the people who crucified him, then what's my excuse? You commanded me in your word to forgive so I make the decision to do so today. Lord, strengthen me so I can do the right thing. Lord, get any impurities out of my heart. I decree that I will forgive them and let it go. I bless my enemies. Thank you for answering this prayer in Jesus name. Amen.

TWENTY THREE

Challenge Nineteen

Faith Declaration Of The Day: The prayers of the righteous avails much (James 5:16). If I ask anything according to God's will I can be confident that he hears me (1 John 5:14). Today I declare that God's abundance is surrounding my life and that my life is marked by excellence and integrity.

Today's Passage: Read 2 Chronicles 6:11-42

In today's passage we read about how King Solomon gathers the people together and leads them in a prayer of dedication for the new temple. He starts his prayer exalting God and reminding Him of His promises. This prayer consists of several things. Solomon asked God to watch over the temple, to bring justice in the temple, asked for forgiveness for his people if they sinned against Him, and reminds God of His sovereignty. We also see that Solomon reminds God of the covenant that He made with his father David.

God is a God of covenant. He wants to honor and establish His covenant with you. When you pray, remind God of His many promises that apply to your situation. Just as Solomon dedicated the temple to God, you can dedicate your fleshly temple or body unto the Lord. God longs to dwell with you. He thinks about you constantly. As long as you pray the will of God concerning your life, then God's promises are always yes and Amen. Remember to praise God, lifting Him up, then the blessings will follow.

Dear Heavenly Father,

I praise you. I lift your name on High! You are so worthy. You are the God who establishes your covenant with your people. I ask you to establish your covenant of peace and prosperity with me today. I dedicate my life and my body to you! Use me Lord for your Glory. I surrender everything to you. I repent of my sins and I ask you to wash me in the blood of Jesus Christ. Thank you for answering this prayer in Jesus name. Amen.

TWENTY FOUR

Challenge Twenty

Faith Declaration Of The Day: Prayer changes things. I will speak life over my circumstances. I will thank God for the end results. Today I declare 2 Thessalonians 3:16 that The Lord of peace himself will give me peace at all times in every way. May The Lord be with me.

Today's Passage: Read 2 Chronicles 20:1-23

In today's passage we read about how God caused the enemies of Jehoshaphat to destroy themselves. Initially, the King was afraid when three different enemies tried to attack him at once. He gathered all the people together to fast and pray. As they sought the Lord, He spoke through a prophet with certain instructions and words of comfort. After, the word of the Lord came, everyone worshipped the Lord. As they followed God's instructions and begin to praise Him, He ambushed their enemies.

Maybe you are in an overwhelming situation. It may appear that you will be defeated and not come out victorious. However, the battle is not yours but the Lord's. As you add fasting to your prayer life, God will give you various instructions, bless you, and defeat your enemies. Fasting with prayer is a double threat to the enemy or devil. If you add praise to this equation, it becomes a triple threat to the enemy. Don't get distracted by the storms around you because it's not your battle but the Lord's.

Dear Heavenly Father,

I give you praise. I bow down and worship you. I thank you in advance for answering my prayers. I am so encouraged to know that you will protect and defend me. I am so grateful to know that you will bless me as I follow your instructions. I make a commitment to live a fasted lifestyle. I decree that I am victorious everywhere I go because you are with me. I decree that as I praise you, Lord, you will ambush my enemies and it will be a sweat less battle for me. Thank you for answering this prayer in Jesus name. Amen.

TWENTY FIVE

Challenge Twenty One

Faith Declaration Of The Day: Prayer is the key to the heart of God. Prayer is one of the way to a real and personal relationship with God. "The earnest prayer of a righteous person has great power and wonderful results" (James 5:16). Today I declare that God has the solutions to every problem I will ever face already lined up. I declare that God will place the right people and the right breaks in my future.

Today's Passage: Read Ezra 8:21-23

In today's passage we read about how the prophet Ezra proclaimed a fast and prayed a prayer of protection. He needed God to protect the Jews on their return to Jerusalem. They were an open target for robbers on their voyage and he was too ashamed to ask the King for military protection since he told the King about the power and wrath of God. So Ezra and the Jews prayed and fasted and trusted the Lord to protect them on their journey and God answered their prayers.

You may have fasted and prayed about a situation, now you need to trust God to answer your prayers. He is so faithful. God honors His word above His name. God can supernatural protect you just as he did for Ezra and the Jews. Sometimes in life you may face impossible situations. There is no way humanly possible you can get out of your dilemma yourself. Only God can do this for you. As you fast and pray, God will add the supernatural on your natural efforts.

Dear Heavenly Father,

I repent of my sins. I come before you with my whole heart. Lord, you know what I have need of before I even ask you. I ask you to protect, strengthen, provide, guide, and bless me today. I know that my fasting and prayer is not in vain. Lord, I am believing you for so much. There is no way that I can make certain things happen but I trust that you can. I thank you in advance for the open doors. I cancel every assignment from the enemy against me in Jesus name. Amen.

TWENTY SIX

Challenge Twenty Two

Faith Declaration Of The Day: Prayer and the Word of God are food for my soul. God loves for me to talk to Him. He thinks about me constantly. The prayers of the upright are His delight (Proverbs 15:8). Today I declare that unexpected blessings are coming my way and God will open up supernatural doors for me.

Today's Passage: Read Nehemiah 9

In today's passage we read about how the people confessed their sins and their ancestor's sins before God. They fasted and wore sackcloth garments which represented their grief. Then they began to read out of the book of the law. They began this prayer by exalting God and reminding him all of his promises. They also recalled all the Lord's mighty acts that he performed and about his great compassion.

Maybe you need God to move for you in your situation. God will not despise your prayer if you repent and confess your sins. Some of your blessings are held up because of generational sins. You can stand in the gap and repent of the sins from your ancestors. You can remind God of His faithfulness and recall the many countless acts of testimonies. Remember to humble yourself from time to time with fasting and God will answer your petition.

Dear Heavenly Father,

I honor and praise you. I thank you for all your wonders in the earth. I am so encouraged by all the many testimonies. I humble myself before you. I repent of my sins and the sins of my ancestors. I repent of the sins of my nation. I confess that you are the true living God. There is nobody like you Lord. I ask that you forgive us our sins this day. Lord have mercy upon us. I ask that you show up in our lives in a mighty way. Thank you, for answering this prayer in Jesus name. Amen.

TWENTY SEVEN
Challenge Twenty Three

Faith Declaration Of The Day: God takes delight in his children's prayers. The steps of a good man are ordered by The Lord; and he delights in his way (Psalm 37:23). Today I declare that God will give me the desires of my heart because I delight myself in him.

Today's Passage: Read Psalm 44

In today's passage we read a prayer for help, or a lamentation. The sons of Korah were crying out to God for help because they were overwhelmed by the things that were happening around them. They also felt like God had forsaken them. As they cried out to God, they confessed that how He helped them in the past and how they trusted Him. They reminded God that they have remained faithful. They also humbled themselves by lying flat on the ground in the dirt.

It may seem like you have prayed and prayed over again about a situation and God is not moving. It may feel like God isn't hearing your prayers and he will never answer you. Sometimes the pain is necessary to birth greatness. Sometimes the pathway of brokenness is way to your miracle. When you feel overwhelmed by the trials in life, reflect back on all the things God has done. You will begin to trust God and have a deep inner sense that God will come through for you. Hold tight. Your answer to your prayers are on the way.

Dear Heavenly Father,

I exalt you. I give you me. I give you all the pain and frustrations in life. I give you my whole heart. I don't understand why I have to suffer sometimes. However, I refuse to allow this storm to overwhelm me. Lord, I am crying out for help with everything within me. I know that you will never forsake me. I know that you will not leave me in despair. Lord, please make haste to help me. Come quickly Lord on my behalf. I have remained faithful to your word. Remember me God. Thank you, for answering this prayer in Jesus name. Amen.

TWENTY EIGHT

Challenge Twenty Four

Faith Declaration Of The Day: I will keep on praying. Oh, taste and see that The Lord is good; blessed is the man that trusts in Him! Those who seek The Lord shall not lack any good thing (Psalm 34). Today I declare that God will open up the windows of heaven and pour me out an abundance of blessings.

Today's Passage: Read Psalm 60

In today's passage we read a prayer for help or a lamentation. The people cried out to God after being defeated. They felt like God had rejected them and scattered them. They knew that they were not able to defeat their enemies in their own strength.

They needed God to intervene immediately. They reminded God of His own spoken words.

You may have just received bad news or things did not work out the way you intended them too. You may be flooded with fear and doubt. You may even feel like God is mad at you. However, none of that is true. God loves you and He promises in His word to fight for you. This is not the time to fall apart and to give up. This is the time to cry out to God in prayer and stand on the promises in the bible. If you believe God with everything within you, He will come through for you. It comes down to faith. Your faith will cause God to move.

Dear Heavenly Father,

You are so great. I will continue to praise you regardless of how I feel. I humble myself before you. God, I need you with every fiber of my being. I cannot fight this battle on my own. I need you to intervene. I need you to deliver me from the enemy. I need a turnaround in my life. Lord, strengthen me and answer me this day. I will testify of your goodness in all the earth. Thank you for answering this prayer in Jesus name. Amen.

TWENTY NINE

Challenge Twenty Five

Faith Declaration Of The Day: I will PUSH. I will pray until something happens. Matthew 7:7-8 says, Ask and it will be given to you; seek and you will find; knock and the door will be opened to you. For everyone who asks receives; the one who seeks finds; and to the one who knocks, the door will be opened. Today I declare Psalm 90:17 that the favor of the Lord our God be upon us, and establish the work of our hands upon us; yes, establish the work of our hands!

Today's Passage: Read Psalm 80

In today's passage we read a prayer for God to bring Israel back or restore them. They exalted God and reminded Him of him sovereignty. They asked Him, how long will you be mad at us? They confessed that they were in a time of suffering and sorrow and how much they needed Him. They asked the Lord to extend His kindness and to take them back. They made a vow unto God that they will not depart from His ways if He restored them.

You may be going through a tough time. You may have lots of questions that you need answers to. It is okay to ask God questions. God will give you clarity and direction as you cry out to Him. You may have messed up in life; however, God is the God of multiple chances. As you cry out to God, He will restore you first back unto Himself then other areas of your life. Sometimes, in that dark place, the vows you make unto the Lord will cause Him to move mightily on your behalf. Remember to honor the vows you made to God after he blesses you.

Dear Heavenly Father,
I exalt you. I humble myself in your presence. I come to you and I confess my many sins. I repent and I ask you to restore me God. Lord, deepen our relationship. Restore my joy, peace, hope, dreams, and everything else that I lost. Help me God. You are worthy and only you can fix my situation. I promise that I will honor you and testify of your goodness all the days of my life. Thank you for answering this prayer in Jesus name. Amen.

THIRTY

Challenge Twenty Six

Faith Declaration Of The Day: As I pray today, I am getting stronger and stronger and the enemy is getting weaker and weaker. Much prayer helps keep the devil away. I will humble myself, submit to God, resist the devil and he will flee. Today I declare that I will stay in the safety and will of God for my life. I declare that I will draw near to God and he will draw near to me.

Today's Passage: Read Luke 1:8-17

In today's passage we read the story of Zechariah or Elizabeth's husband serving as a priest. Crowds of people were praying outside of the temple. Zechariah was chosen to burn the incense that hour. During his duty, an angel appeared to him telling him that God had heard his prayer and that he would have a son named John the Baptist. The angel promised that God would use John in a great way. Zechariah was in the right posture to have a move of God in his life.

As you posture yourself and stay in God's will, you will see the miraculous. You will always have an open heaven over your head. As you serve God and remain faithful to Him, He will give you your heart's desires. Zechariah and Elizabeth were old but God blessed them to have a child. They thought this was impossible. Nothing is too hard for God. Don't let lost time make you feel like God still can't bless you. God will withhold no good thing from you if you walk uprightly.

Dear Heavenly Father,

You are so faithful. There is nothing too hard for you. I know that you delight in the prayers of the upright. You long to be good to your children. Lord, I place every desire that I have on the altar and believe that you will bless me. Lord, I trust you even when it hurts and I don't understand. Restore the years that the locust has eaten. I am so thankful that you will make up for lost time. Thank you for making my latter days better than my former days in Jesus name. Amen.

THIRTY ONE
Challenge Twenty Seven

Faith Declaration Of The Day: I will press as I pray. No weapon formed against me will prosper and I have the victory wherever I go. Today I declare that God will supply all my needs according to His riches and Glory in Christ Jesus.

Today's Passage: Read Acts 3:1-10

In today's passage we read the story about how John and Peter went to the temple every day to pray. They had a strong prayer life and the power of God flowed through them. There was a man that was crippled all his life that came across their paths. The man begged them for money but Peter replied that instead of giving him money, he would give him something else. Then

Peter commanded his healing in the name of Jesus. The man began to walk and was healed. All the people started praising God for his miracle because they knew he used to be crippled.

As you develop a consistent prayer life, you will see the power of God flow through you. God longs to do signs and wonders through you for His Glory. Just as the crippled man had an impossible and long-term situation that was changed by the power of God, so can your situation be turned around. Continue to command things to change for the better in the name of Jesus. Walk in the authority of Jesus Christ. You are His child. Believe God for the miraculous and God will come through for you.

Dear Heavenly Father,

You are worthy. I thank you that you are the God who performs many miracles and wonders. I make myself available to you. Lord, use me in a mighty way. I decree that I will develop a strong prayer life and will make the sacrifice to seek you daily. Lord, I want to see your power flow through me and bless the lives of people that cross my path. Thank you for answering this prayer in Jesus name. Amen.

THRITY TWO

Challenge Twenty Eight

Faith Declaration Of The Day: As I pray today, I will focus my mind on Jesus and will have perfect peace in the midst of troubles that I face. God will provide all my needs and I will not have any lack. Today I declare Joel 2:25-26 that God will restore everything I lost and he will perform miracles in my life.

Today's Scripture: Read Acts 16:16-18

In today's passage we read the story about Paul, Silas, and the lady with an evil spirit. Paul and Silas had a strong prayer life. The power of God flowed through them strongly. As they were going to find a place to pray, a lady with a spirit of divination followed them. She was involved in fortune telling and her owners made a lot of money off her. She followed them for days telling people they were men of the Most High God and they are telling people how to be saved. This lady started to annoy Apostle Paul, so he turned around and commanded the evil spirit to leave her. The spirit left that hour.

As you build up your prayer life, the power of God will flow through you as never before. You will start to see more manifestations of God operating in your life. You will realize the authority that Jesus has giving you and you will begin to walk in it on a higher level. You will cast out devils and heal the sick in the name of Jesus. You will become the oracle of God as He uses you in the earth as a mighty sign and wonder. You will speak to those mountains or impossibilities in your life and see them crumble.

Dear Heavenly Father,
I exalt you. Lord, give me the spirit of prayer and develop a stronger prayer life in me. Lord, I want to be consistent in praying. Lord, I humble myself and I want to be used by you. I yield my body to you as an instrument of righteousness. I desire to have your presence flow through me. I decree that I will walk in the authority of Jesus Christ. I will cast out devils and heal the sick in your name. Thank you for answering this prayer in Jesus name. Amen.

THIRTY THREE

Challenge Twenty Nine

Faith Declaration Of The Day: I will keep PUSHing (Pray until something happens). Matthew 21:22 says, "And whatever you ask in prayer, you will receive, if you have faith." I declare that every mountain that is blocking my path be removed and cast into the sea in Jesus' name.

Today's Scripture: Read Acts 16:25-34

In today's passage we read the story about how after Paul casts out an evil spirit, he and Silas are beaten and arrested because the owners of the lady with the divination spirit can no longer make money off her. At midnight, they began praying and praising God. All of a sudden an earthquake occurred, the doors opened and everyone's chains fell off. The prisoner guard was about to kill himself when he thought everyone had escaped. But Paul shouted and told him that they were still there and not to kill himself. The prisoner knew that God was real, and he got saved. He confessed Jesus as Lord and Savior.

You may be in a spiritual, mental, or physically prison. However, God is with you just as He was with Paul and Silas. As you begin to sing songs to God and praise Him, miracles will break out. Your prayers are powerful to cause an earthquake in the spirit and God will shift things in your favor. As you praise God, every yoke of oppression and demonic bondage will break off your life. Your praise will give you a divine turnaround. After you prayed about the situation, switch to praise.

Dear Heavenly Father,

I give you praise. I ask you to put a new song in my mouth. I will praise you when it hurts. I will praise you in the good times. I will praise you in the bad times. I decree that I am victorious. I command every demonic yoke to break off my life in the name of Jesus. I plead the blood of Jesus upon myself. I thank you in advance for giving me a mighty breakthrough in Jesus name. Amen.

THIRTY FOUR

Challenge Thirty

Faith Declaration Of The Day: Glory to God! I have completed this challenge. I decree that I have developed a deeper level of intimacy with God and that my prayer life has gone to another level. I will draw near to God He will draw near to me. I declare that since I seek first God and His righteousness that everything else will be added unto me.

Today's Scripture: Read 1 Samuel 1:1-20

In today's passage we read the story about how Hannah was sad because she wanted to have a child. Her husband's other wife, Peninnah was very cruel to her and mocked her for not having any children. Hannah went to the temple to pray. As she prayed she wept bitterly that the priest thought she was drunk. She told him that she wasn't drunk, and the priest blessed her. God remembered her, and she conceived Samuel.

You may be desperate and really need a move of God. Just as Hannah made a vow to give God back her son so you can make a vow unto God to use your blessing for His Glory. Hannah's tears were prayers because she could barely speak. As she prayed no words were coming out. Every tear that you have shed are tears as well. God sees your heart, and He knows your every need and concern. God is so faithful and He will give you the desires of your heart as you delight yourself in Him.

Dear Heavenly Father,

I come to you today. I humble myself and I give you all the brokenness. I am so desperate for a miracle. God, you are the only one who has the power to change my situation. Lord, if you don't bless me then no one can. I trust you. I choose believe that you have my best interest at hand. I believe that everything will work out for my good. I decree that my manifestation of my blessing is here in Jesus name. God remember me this day. Amen.

ABOUT THE AUTHOR

Kimberly Hargraves is a highly sought after prophetic voice, Intercessor and a prolific author. There is no doubt that she has a global mandate on her life to serve the nations of the world by spreading the Gospel of Jesus Christ. She has a quickly expanding worldwide healing and deliverance ministry. Kimberly Hargraves wears many hats to fulfill the call God has placed on her life as an entrepreneur over several businesses including her own personal brand Rejoice Essentials which promotes the Gospel of Jesus Christ. This brand includes a magazine and anointing oils. She also serves as a life coach and mentor to many women. She is also the loving mother of two wonderful children. Kimberly has dedicated her life to the work of ministry and to serve others under the call God has placed over her life. Kimberly currently resides in Colorado.

She is a very anointed woman of God who signs, miracles and wonders follow. The miraculous and incessant testimonies attributed to her ministry are incalculable, with many reporting physical and mental healing, financial breakthroughs, debt cancellations and other favorable outcomes. She is known across the globe as a servant who truly labors on behalf of God's people through intercession. God blessed her to start her ministry to help encourage others. God used her pain to reveal her writing ability and to do his work. God blessed her to write about life experiences and give a message of hope to others with broken hearts.

She is the author of The Following:

"Overcoming Difficult Life Experiences with Scriptures and Prayers"

"Overcoming Emotions with Prayers"

"Daily Prayers That Bring Changes"

"In Right Standing,"

"Obedience Is Key,"

"Prayers That Break The Yoke Of The Enemy: A Book Of Declarations,"

"Prayers That Demolish Demonic Strongholds: A Book Of Declarations,"

"Work Smarter. Not Harder. A Book Of Declarations For The Workforce,"

"Set The Captives Free: A Book Of Deliverance."

"Pray More Challenge"

"Empowering The New Me: Fifty Tips To Becoming A Godly Woman"

You can find more about Kimberly at www.kimberlyhargraves.com. Follow Kimberly on Facebook at https://www.facebook.com/seerprophetesskimberlyhargraves/.

Follow Kimberly on Twitter and periscope @SeerProphetessK.

Index

A

Abraham, 42–43
altar, 30–31, 54, 63, 82
angels, 9, 12, 40–41, 61–62, 81
anointing, 13
assignment, 3, 61–62, 72
atmosphere, 20, 56
authority, 15, 24, 56, 84, 86

B

Baal, 30–32
battle, 50, 70, 78
believers, 55–56
birthing position, 27–28
bless, 12, 14, 17, 19, 24, 45–47, 54, 58, 62, 64–66, 70, 72, 80, 82, 84
blessings, 23–24, 26, 53, 61, 66, 68, 74, 77, 90
blood, 9, 56, 58, 62, 68, 88
bondage, 18
brokenness, 36, 62, 76, 90

C

captivity, 18, 57
cast, 38, 49, 86–87
ceasing, 4, 28
Chronicles, 10, 20, 67, 69
city, 17, 36, 42–43, 58
commandments, 12, 38, 53, 58
commands, 12, 22, 24–25, 28, 31, 37, 84, 88
confess, 8–10, 52, 66, 74, 80
confidence, 15–17
covenant, 34, 68
curse, 2, 19

D

deceptions, 32
decree, 12, 20, 26–27, 29–30, 32–33, 39–45, 50, 52–53, 55, 62, 64, 66, 70, 84, 88–90
delight, 39, 46, 73, 75, 82, 90
deliverance, 39, 41, 43, 50, 92
devil, 8, 19–21, 24, 70, 81, 86
doors, 20, 44, 87
dreams, 44–45, 80

E

earthquake, 87–88
Elijah, 27–28, 31–32
enemies, 4–5, 13, 15, 19–20, 24–25, 36, 46, 49, 56, 66, 69–70, 72, 77–78, 81, 92

evil, 9, 44
evil spirit, 85–87

F

faith, 1, 8–9, 13–14, 20, 22–23, 25–29, 31, 41, 47, 60, 78, 87
faithfulness, 36, 42, 74
falseness, 32
fasting, 19–20, 45, 70, 72, 74
Father, 9, 19
forgiveness, 18–19, 39, 47, 52, 54, 58, 66–67
forsaken, 46–47, 58, 75

G

glory, 12, 15, 31, 35, 47, 49, 68, 83–84, 89–90
gospel, 39, 55–56, 58, 91

H

Hannah, 16, 89–90
harvest, 25, 53
healing, 10, 43, 55, 84
heart, 2, 8, 17, 30, 35–36, 39, 46–47, 52, 55, 66, 71–72, 75–76, 82, 90
heaven, 8–10, 19, 31, 39, 56, 64, 77
Hezekiah, 35–36
Holy Spirit, 7, 9, 14–17, 21, 56, 64
honor, 8–9, 32, 34, 44, 68, 74, 80

humble, 10, 18, 32, 34, 52, 54, 58, 60, 64, 66, 74, 78, 80–81, 86, 90

humility, 18, 52, 59

I

idols, 33

intercession, 34, 39, 43, 57, 91

intercessors, 5, 91

J

Jesus, 8, 24, 26, 42, 50, 52–53, 56, 61, 63–66, 84–86, 88

joy, 9, 25, 48, 59–60, 80

L

laws, 34, 73

Lord, 2–3, 5, 7–9, 11–12, 22–23, 25–26, 28–30, 33–34, 36–40, 43–47, 52, 58–60, 62–66, 68–70, 74–80

Lord's prayer, 63–64

M

mercy, 34, 39, 43, 47, 49–50, 52, 58, 66, 74

ministry, 91

miracles, 12, 28–29, 31, 41, 55–56, 76, 84–85, 88, 90–91

money, 13, 17, 20, 83, 86–87

mountains, 33, 86–87

N

nation, 4, 39, 57–58, 74, 91

P

pain, 5, 36, 47, 62, 76, 91
Paul, 53–54, 85, 87–88
peace, 5, 23, 25, 47–48, 50, 60, 65, 69, 80
Peter, 24, 40–41, 49, 55–56, 83–84
power of God, 25, 83–86
praise, 9, 20, 22–23, 29, 34, 41, 45–47, 49, 59, 68, 70, 74, 78, 88
prayer life, 1, 64, 70, 86, 89
praying, 1, 3, 5, 11–12, 18–21, 28, 41, 45, 61, 77, 81, 86–87
promises, 11, 15–16, 23, 31, 34, 47, 58, 60, 67–68, 73, 78, 80
prophets, 5, 16, 30–32, 35–36, 54, 69
prostrate, 11, 15
protection, 49–50, 71

R

refuge, 35, 50, 57
release, 47, 55–56
repent, 10, 32, 34, 36, 39, 41, 45, 47, 50, 52, 54, 60, 64, 72, 74
repentance, 9–10, 51
riches, 12, 35, 44, 49, 83
righteous, 38–39, 43

S

sacrifice, 14, 22, 31, 43, 45, 84
secret, 19, 43, 63
servant, 27–28, 91
sins, 4, 8–10, 24, 32, 34, 36, 39, 41, 47, 52, 54, 57, 60, 64, 72–74
sovereignty, 67, 80
strengthen, 61–62, 64, 66, 72, 78
supernatural, 13–14, 25, 72
surrender, 9, 25, 41, 62, 64, 68

T

temple, 67–68, 81, 83, 89
temptation, 24, 61–62
testimonies, 47, 74
time, 2–3, 5, 7, 11, 13, 16, 23, 28, 36, 43, 45, 53–54, 74, 78, 80
tongues, 9, 12, 20–21
trials, 2, 14, 37, 40, 42, 62, 76
trust, 4, 16–17, 25, 32, 34, 43, 54, 72, 77, 82, 90

U

un-forgiveness, 17–19

V

victorious, 11, 50, 70, 88

victory, 20, 32, 83
vision, 15–16, 41
vows, 37, 80, 90

W

wall, 5, 35, 43
weapons, 15, 56, 83
weary, 11, 53
wisdom, 24, 44–45
worries, 41–42
worship, 9, 15, 25, 31, 33, 41, 44–45, 70

Y

yoke, 13, 88, 92

Z

Zechariah, 81–82

[Created with TExtract / www.Texyz.com]

www.ingramcontent.com/pod-product-compliance
Lightning Source LLC
Chambersburg PA
CBHW071529080526
44588CB00011B/1606